CARTA'S ILLUSTRATED BIBLE ATLAS

WITH HISTORICAL NOTES
BY F. F. BRUCE

Carta, Jerusalem

TABLE OF CONTENTS

Second Revised Edition
Copyright © 1994, 2010, 2015 by Carta Jerusalem, Ltd.

ISBN: 978-965-220-812-5
Printed in Israel

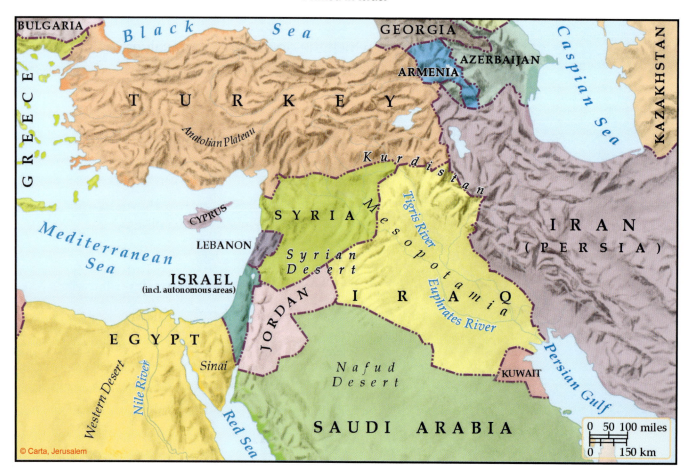

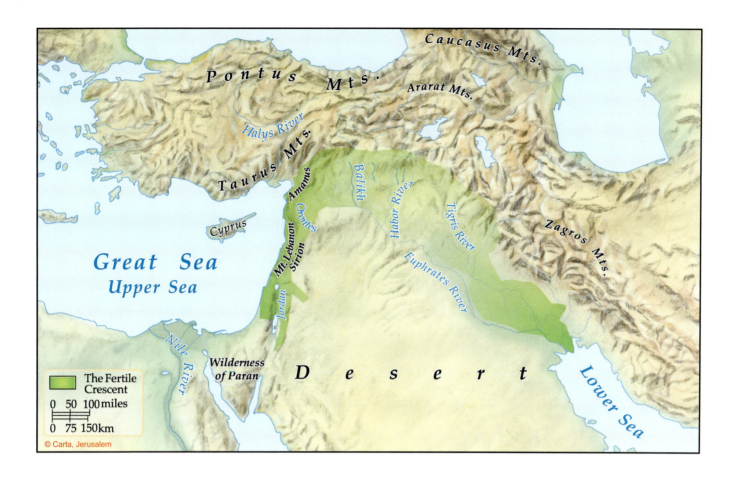

FOREWORD

This Atlas is designed as an aid to the study of the Bible. The contents of the Bible are so closely related to the lands or cities in which the recorded events took place, and in which the documents themselves were written, that it helps greatly to know something about those lands and cities. This is one kind of knowledge that the Atlas provides.

Moreover, the writing of the books of the Bible spans a period of some 1,400 years, and the history which they record reaches back to the beginnings of civilization in the ancient Near East. To understand them properly, it is necessary to have some knowledge of the historical as well as the geographical setting. The maps are arranged in historical sequence, and the notes are intended to relate the Bible story to its historical background.

A further, and very useful, aid is supplied by the chronological table.

F. F. Bruce

ANCI
SECONI

Empire of Hammurabi, early 18th cent. B.C.

Egyptian sphere of influence

Empire of Thutmose III, c.1468 B.C.

Minoan–Mycenaean sphere

Hittite sphere

Invasion of Sea Peoples, 12th cent. B.C.

Noph City of importance

| 0 | 100 | 200 | 300 miles |
| 0 | 100 | 200 | 300 | 400 km |

© Carta, Jerusalem

PALACE AT MARI
(18th century B.C.)

Scribal School

Great Courtyard

Old Palace

Royal Quarters

Throne-room

Chapel

Workshops

Storerooms

| 0 | 20 | 40 | 60 yards |
| 0 | 20 | 40 m |

Hammurabi

The second millennium B.C. was a great imperial age in the ancient Near East. In the Euphrates-Tigris valley the Assyrian and Babylonian empires enjoyed periods of expansion with alternating periods of weakness. On the Middle Euphrates the kingdom of Mari (18th century B.C.) extended its authority into Syria. Later, the kingdom of Mitanni flourished in the Upper Euphrates valley: its ruler was sufficiently important to correspond with the king of Egypt as an equal. The two dominant empires for most of the millennium, however, were those of the Egyptians and the Hittites.

The Egyptians enjoyed two periods of power- the Middle Kingdom (Dynasty XII) from about 1991 to 1786 B.C., and the New Kingdom (Dynasties XVIII and XIX) from about 1560 to 1200 B.C. Between these two phases Egypt was invaded and dominated by Semites from Asia, known as the Hyksos.

The kingdom of the Hittites, established in Asia Minor soon after 2000 B.C., became an imperial power and extended its rule south into Syria, reaching its zenith under Suppiluliumas (c. 1380–1350 B.C.). As the Egyptian rulers of Dynasty XVIII extended their power northward, they came

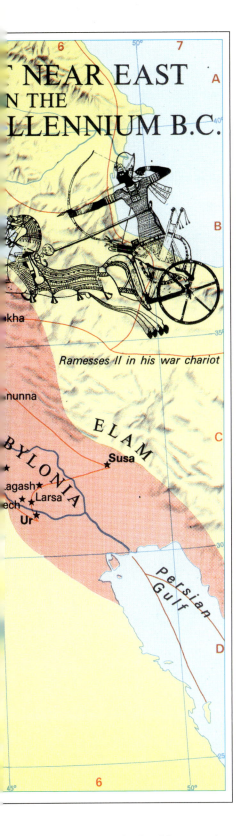

NEAR EAST
N THE
LLENNIUM B.C.

Ramesses II in his war chariot

Egyptan warship, 1200 B.C.

Thutmose III

into contact with the Hittites, their relations being sometimes diplomatic and sometimes hostile. A battle was fought between the two empires in 1286 B.C. at Kedesh on the Orontes in Syria; it was followed by a treaty confirming the Orontes as the frontier between their spheres of interest. The treaty was cemented by the marriage of a Hittite princess to the Egyptian king Rameses II (of Dynasty XIX).

About 1200 B.C. the Hittite empire collapsed and Egypt began to enter a further period of decline.

In this context are to be set the movements of the Hebrew patriarchs recorded in Genesis and Exodus. Abraham left Ur in southern Mesopotamia and settled for a time in Harran, east of the upper Euphrates; then he moved on to Canaan, where he lived as a pastoral nomad. Once, because of a famine, he paid a short visit to Egypt. His descendants maintained their links with Harran for two generations. Many of them, in a time of prolonged famine, went down from Canaan to Egypt and settled there for four generations. Their departure from Egypt under Moses and their settlement in Canaan under Joshua (c. 1200 B.C.) marked the beginning of Israel's history as a nation.

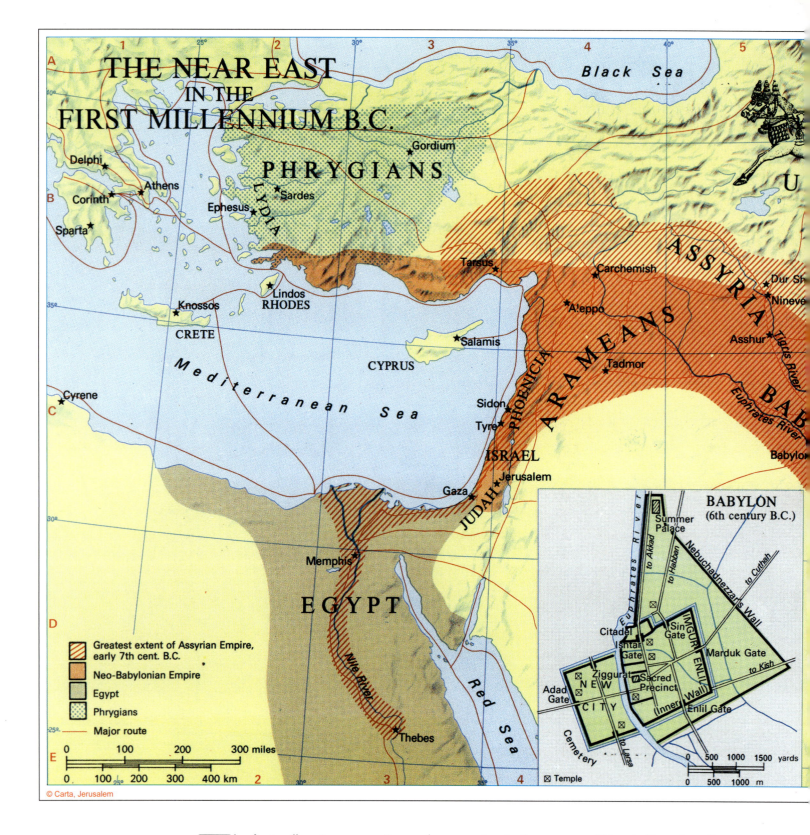

THE NEAR EAST
IN THE
FIRST MILLENNIUM B.C.

PHRYGIANS

Delphi
Athens *Sardes*
Corinth *Ephesus* LYDIA
Sparta

Gordium

Black Sea

ASSYRIA

Tarsus *Carchemish* *Dur Sh*
Aleppo *Nineve*
Asshur

Cyrene

Knossos RHODES
Lindos
CRETE

Salamis

CYPRUS

Tadmor

BAB

Mediterranean Sea

PHOENICIA ARAMEANS

Sidon
Tyre

Babylon

ISRAEL
Jerusalem
Gaza JUDAH

Memphis

EGYPT

Thebes

Red Sea

Greatest extent of Assyrian Empire, early 7th cent. B.C.
Neo-Babylonian Empire
Egypt
Phrygians
Major route

0   100   200   300 miles
0 100 200 300 400 km

BABYLON
(6th century B.C.)

Euphrates River
to Akkad
to Habban Nebuchadnezzar's Wall
Summer Palace
to Cutheh

Citadel
Ishtar Gate
Sin Gate
IMGUR ENLIL Marduk Gate
to Kish

Ziggurat
NEW CITY
Sacred Precinct
Inner Wall
Enlil Gate

Adad Gate

Cemetery *to Larsa*

⊠ Temple

0   500 1000 1500 yards
0   500 1000 m

© Carta, Jerusalem

The first millennium B.C. witnessed a recession in the power of Egypt. Occasionally a powerful king would attempt to reassert Egyptian authority in Canaan. Shishak, for example (of Dynasty XXII), invaded the kingdoms of Judah and Israel about 925 B.C.: one account of his invasion is given in 1 Kings 14:25–28 and another, Shishak's own record, appears in relief on the walls of the temple of Amun at Karnak (Thebes). But he did not maintain control over the territory he invaded.

Between 1000 and 612 B.C. the dominant power in the Near East was Assyria. In 853 B.C. a concerted effort was made by states of Cilicia and Syria (including Israel) to halt the Assyrians' westward advance. They gave battle to the Assyrians at Qarqar on the Orontes and it was twelve years before the Assyrians returned. But when they did return, they proved irresistible. One after another the western kingdoms fell before them: Damascus in 732 B.C., Samaria (Israel) in 721 B.C., while Judah survived as a weak vassal state. At the height of its power the Assyrian Empire extended over Elam (east of the Persian Gulf), Armenia, south-east Asia Minor, Syria and Palestine, and for a short time Egypt itself. Thebes, capital of Upper Egypt, was sacked in 663 B.C.

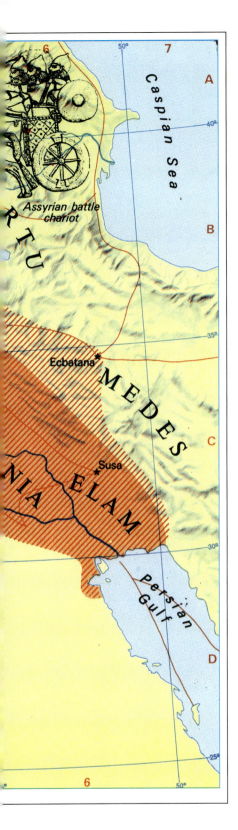

Assyrian battle chariot

Phoenician merchant ship, 7th century B.C.

A Median leading horses

But Assyria was overthrown at last by the Medes from the east and the Babylonians from the south: they divided among themselves the former Assyrian territory. Nineveh fell in 612 B.C. The Egyptians, trying to gain some advantage for themselves from this new turn of events, were defeated in 605 B.C. at Carchemish on the Euphrates by the Babylonians, who established control as far as the frontier of Egypt.

The Median kingdom lasted for 63 years after the fall of Nineveh; then it fell in its turn before Cyrus, ruler of a small kingdom on the Persian Gulf and founder of the Persian Empire. In a few years Cyrus, having secured sovereignty over the dual monarchy of the Medes and Persians, pushed his empire west to the Aegean Sea. Then he captured Babylon in 539 B.C. He is commemorated in the Bible for his edict authorizing the return of the Jews who had been exiled from their homeland by the Babylonians. His son Cambyses conquered Egypt in 525 B.C. The Persian Empire stood for 200 years, stretching "from India to Ethiopia" (Esther 1:1); it was finally overthrown by Alexander the Great (331 B.C.).

Rameses II

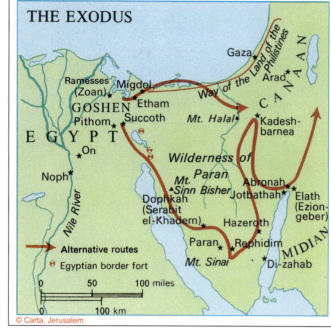

THE EXODUS

Gaza

Ramesses (Zoan)   Migdol

Etham

GOSHEN

Pithom   Succoth

EGYPT

On

Noph

Way of the Land of the Philistines

Arad

CANAAN

Mt. Halal

Kadesh-barnea

Wilderness of Paran

Mt. Sinn Bisher   Abronah

Dophkah (Serabit el-Khadem)   Jotbathah   Elath (Ezion-geber)

Hazeroth

Paran   Rephidim

MIDIAN

Mt. Sinai   Di-zahab

→ Alternative routes
⊕ Egyptian border fort

0   50   100 miles
0   100 km

© Carta, Jerusalem

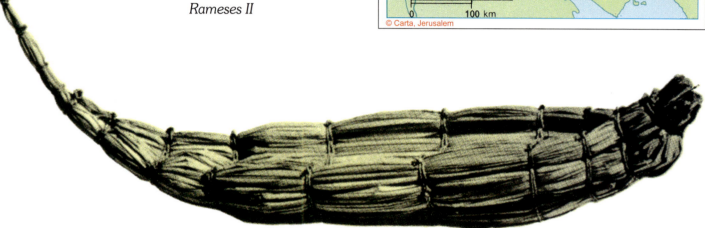

Egyptian reed boat

THE TABERNACLE

Model of the Tabernacle

The main body of the Israelites that left Egypt under Moses moved east through the Wilderness of Zin and then north through Transjordan. Those who advanced north west from Kadesh-barnea into the Negev did not necessarily turn back, as might be inferred from the map: after the defeat of the king of Arad at Hormah (Numbers 21:1–3) some members of the tribe of Judah and their local allies probably consolidated their position and penetrated farther, in the direction of Hebron.

Turning west from Transjordan, the main body crossed the Jordan opposite Jericho. After capturing that citadel, they penetrated into the central highlands, from which some turned north to the Plain of Jezreel and others turned south-west, defeating a coalition of Canaanite kings at the battle of Beth-horon. A minor branch of the body that entered Transjordan advanced north instead of crossing the Jordan and occupied the Amorite territories south and north of the Jabbok.

The areas of settlement did not include the plains, which the Canaanite city-states continued to dominate with their iron-reinforced chariotry. The power of the Canaanites in the Plain of Jezreel was weakened by an Israelite victory won at the river Kishon c. 1125 B.C. But the Israelites were continually menaced by bedouin from the east and, more seriously, by Philistines from the western seaboard. The Philistines, who were immigrants from the Aegean area, gradually extended their control over most of the land west of the Jordan.

For most of this period the tribes of Israel were too disunited to take effective action against their enemies. Their central sanctuary at Shiloh, in Ephraimite territory, housed the ark of the covenant, the symbol of their religious unity, but its role as a cohesive influence was limited. The "judges" who give their name to the book of Judges, which deals with the two centuries between the Israelites' early settlement and the rise of the monarchy, exercised authority for the most part over limited areas.

THE COMING
OF THE
ISRAELITES

Philistine warrior

Fortress of "The Canaan"
Egyptian name for Gaza

THE WALLS OF JERICHO
(7th to late 2nd millennia B.C.)

Cemetery area

Later Canaanite walls

Early Canaanite walls

Neolithic tower

Spring

Middle Canaanite buildings

Modern road

0   20   40   60 yards
0   20   40 m

Map labels:

Mediterranean Sea

Litani River
Ijon
Tyre
Mt. Hermon
DAN
Dan
Kedesh
ASHER
NAPHTALI
Hazor
Bashan
Waters of Merom
Chinnereth
Sea of Chinnereth
Ashtaroth
Geshur
Mt. Carmel
Achshaph
SHAMGAR
ZEBULUN
BARAK
DEBORAH
Yarmuk River
Edrei
Dor
ELON
GIDEON
Ophrah
Mt. Tabor
Kamon
Megiddo
Taanach
Mt. Gilboa
Beth-shean
JAIR
Ramoth-gilead
Plain of Sharon
ISSACHAR
Gilead
MANASSEH
Shamir
Zaphon
TOLA
Shechem
JEPHTAH
Pirathon
Jabbok River
Eben-ezer
ABDON
Jordan River
Aphek
Shiloh
AMMON
EPHRAIM
GAD
Rabbah
EHUD
Bethel
Ai
Gilgal
DAN
Gezer
Jericho
SAMSON
BENJAMIN
Gibeon
Ashdod
Ekron
Zorah
Heshbon
Gath
Jerusalem
Mt. Nebo
Ashkelon
Azekah
Jarmuth
Bethlehem
IBZAN
REUBEN
Gaza
Eglon
Lachish
JUDAH
Hebron
Jahzah
Gerar
Debir
OTHNIEL
Aroer
Dead Sea
Arnon River
Beersheba
Arad
MOAB
Kir-moab
SIMEON
Negeb
Zoar
Zered River
Tamar
Zalmonah
Arabah
Bozrah
Wilderness of Zin
Kadesh-barnea
Punon

Legend

→ The Israelite penetration
(figure) Major battle
(orange box) Limit of Israelite control, 12th cent. B.C.
DAN Israelite Tribe
JAIR Locale of Judge
(square) Philistine city

0   10   20   30   40 miles
0   20   40   60 km

© Carta, Jerusalem

9

The Philistine menace moved the Israelites to choose a king, a military leader for their whole federation. Their choice fell on Saul, a man from the tribe of Benjamin, who gave early promise of deserving their confidence. But in an attempt to restore communications between the central tribes and those in the north, who were cut off from their fellow-Israelites by the Philistine occupation of the Plain of Jezreel, Saul was killed at the battle of Mount Gilboa (c. 1010 B.C.). The Philistines now controlled all Canaan west of the Jordan.

The preservation of Israel's national identity was due to David, a Judaean from Bethlehem, who with his guerrilla force had been for some time in the service of one of the Philistine rulers. With Philistine permission he was installed as king of Judah. When, two years later, Saul's last surviving son was assassinated, all the tribes of Israel invited David to be their king. At first the Philistines raised no objection, thinking that he was still their vassal. But when he strengthened his position by the sudden capture of Jerusalem, which had remained a Canaanite city until now, the Philistines realized that he would threaten their supremacy if he were not immediately crushed. After defeating them in two battles, however, it was David who reduced the Philistines to subjection. Then, by conquest and alliance, he extended his rule until his sphere of influence included all Transjordan and stretched north to the Euphrates.

He bequeathed this minor empire to his son Solomon (c. 970–930 B.C.), whose desire to imitate the style of a great king in his capital at Jerusalem imposed on his people a burden too heavy to bear. By the time of his death most of Israel's subject-nations had regained their independence, and soon after his death his own kingdom split into two parts—the kingdom of Israel in the north and central Canaan and the kingdom of Judah in the south, retaining Jerusalem as its capital.

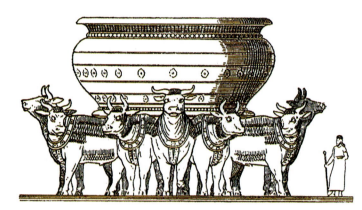

The "Sea" of cast metal

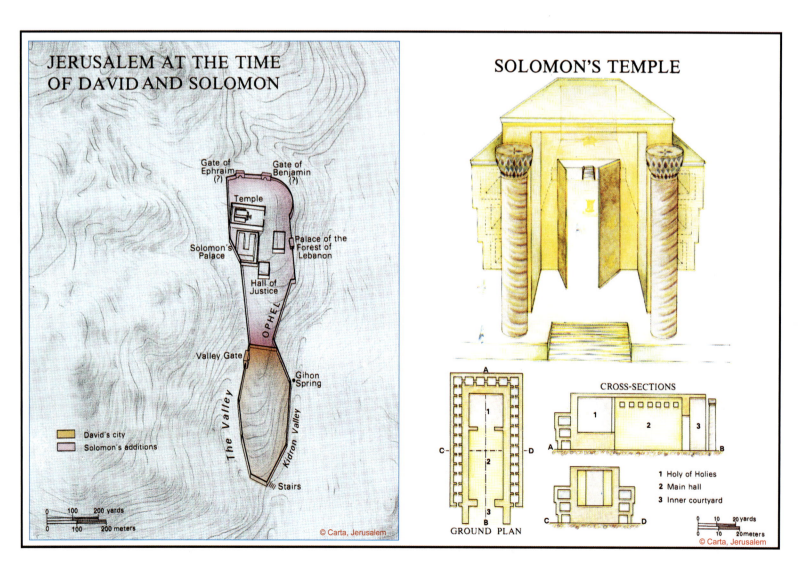

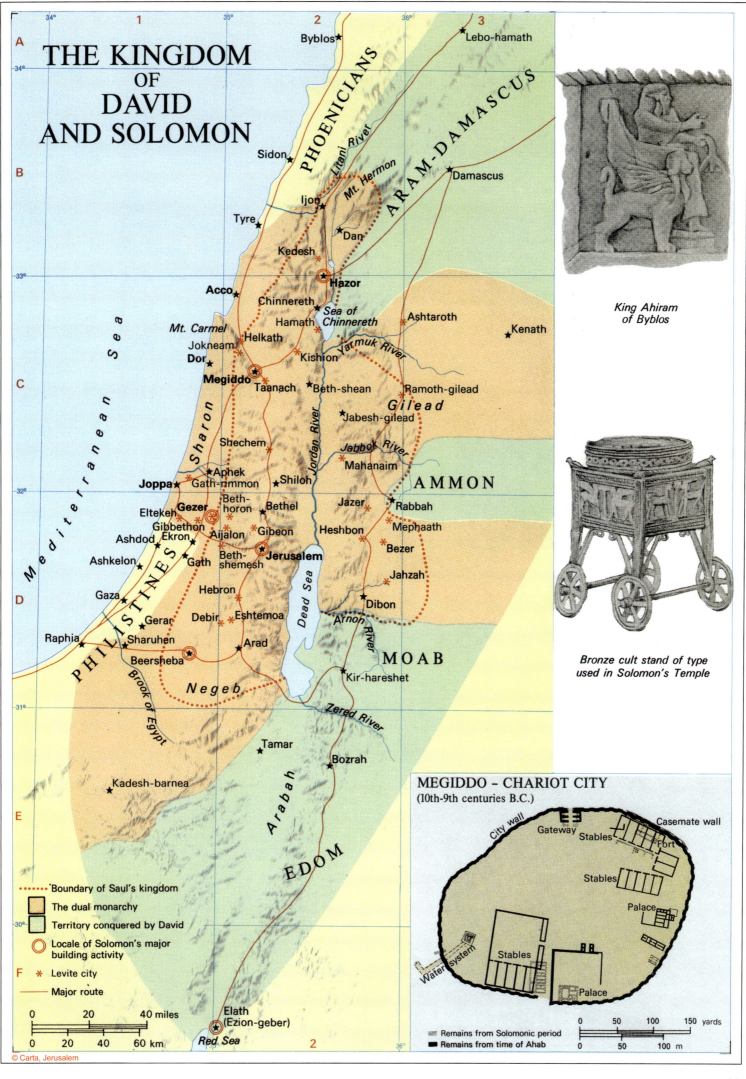

THE KINGDOM OF DAVID AND SOLOMON

Byblos ★

Lebo-hamath ★

PHOENICIANS

ARAM-DAMASCUS

Sidon ★

Damascus ★

Litani River

Mt. Hermon

Ijon ★

Tyre ★

Dan ★

Kedesh ★

Hazor ⊛

Acco ★

Chinnereth ★

Ashtaroth ★

Sea of Chinnereth

Hamath ★

Kenath ★

Mt. Carmel

Helkath ★

Jokneam ★

Kishion ★

Yarmuk River

Dor ★

Megiddo ⊛

Taanach ★

Beth-shean ★

Ramoth-gilead ★

Gilead

Jabesh-gilead ★

Jordan River

Shechem ★

Jabbok River

Mahanaim ★

AMMON

★ Aphek

Sharon

Joppa ★

Gath-rimmon ★

Shiloh ★

Jazer ★

Rabbah ★

Eltekeh ★

Gezer ⊛

Beth-horon ★

Bethel ★

Mephaath ★

Gibbethon ★

Ekron ★

Aijalon ★

Gibeon ★

Heshbon ★

Bezer ★

Ashdod ★

Beth-shemesh ★

Jerusalem ⊛

Ashkelon ★

Gath ★

Jahzah ★

Gaza ★

Hebron ★

Dibon ★

Mediterranean Sea

PHILISTINES

Gerar ★

Debir ★

Eshtemoa ★

Arnon River

Raphia ★

Sharuhen ★

Arad ★

MOAB

Beersheba ⊛

Kir-hareshet ★

Brook of Egypt

Negeb

Zered River

Tamar ★

Bozrah ★

Kadesh-barnea ★

Arabah

EDOM

Dead Sea

Elath (Ezion-geber) ⊛

Red Sea

Legend

- ⋯⋯ Boundary of Saul's kingdom
- ▨ The dual monarchy
- ▨ Territory conquered by David
- ⊛ Locale of Solomon's major building activity
- * Levite city
- — Major route

0   20   40 miles
0   20   40   60 km

King Ahiram of Byblos

Bronze cult stand of type used in Solomon's Temple

MEGIDDO – CHARIOT CITY
(10th–9th centuries B.C.)

City wall

Gateway

Stables

Casemate wall

Fort

Stables

Stables

Palace

Water system

Stables

Palace

0   50   100   150 yards
0   50   100 m

▨ Remains from Solomonic period
▬ Remains from time of Ahab

Assyrian army attacks a city, palace of Tiglath-Pileser III, Calah

The united kingdom of David and Solomon was inevitably weakened by being divided. Almost immediately after the division, both of the succession kingdoms were further weakened by the invasion of the Egyptians under Shishak. Moreover, the two kingdoms waged war with each other for half a century: the dynasty of David in the south did not readily abandon hope of bringing the northern kingdom back under its control.

In the north, one upstart dynasty after another seized power with disconcerting frequency. The strongest of the northern dynasties was founded by Omri, who built a new strategic capital at Samaria (c. 880 B.C.). Under Omri and his successors Israel and Judah were at peace with each other. Judah regained control over Edom, with access to the Gulf of Aqaba; Israel reduced the Transjordanian Moabites to servitude. Israel's great enemy at this time was the Aramaean kingdom of Damascus. But for a year or two even the king of Damascus had to make common cause with Israel (under Omri's son Ahab) to resist the incursion of Shalmaneser III of Assyria; they contributed major contingents to the united army which halted his advance in 853 B.C.

With the fall of the dynasty of Omri (841 B.C.), Israel's position against the Aramaeans was weakened; it seemed at one stage as if they would wipe Israel out. But the damage caused to Damascus by an Assyrian raid in 803 B.C. gave Israel a respite. For the next forty or fifty years both Israel and Judah enjoyed renewed prosperity under Jeroboam II in the north and Uzziah in the south.

This prosperity was brought to an end by fresh attacks from Assyria, which from 745 B.C. onward established its empire over south-western Asia. The kingdoms of Damascus and Samaria were abolished and replaced by Assyrian provinces; the kingdom of Judah escaped a similar fate by the skin of its teeth. The recession of Assyrian power from 625 B.C. onward enabled Josiah, king of Judah, to assert his independence and reform the national religion. But this independence was short-lived. With the fall of Assyria, Babylon became the dominant power in those regions. Had Judah been content to remain tributary to Babylon, it might have survived; as it was, it revolted against Babylon at the instigation of Egypt. In reprisal the Babylonians destroyed Jerusalem and its temple and deported large numbers of the Judaean population to the east (587 B.C.).

The Mesha Stele

THE KINGDOMS OF JUDAH AND ISRAEL

Seal of "Shema servant of Jeroboam"

Map labels:

Byblos
Lebo-hamath
Zarephath
PHOENICIANS
Litani River
ARAM-DAMASCUS
Sidon
Mt. Hermon
Damascus
Tyre
Dan
Kedesh
Bashan
Hazor
Mediterranean Sea
Sea of Chinnereth
Karnaim
Ashtaroth
Rumah
Jezreel Valley
Mt. Carmel
Yarmuk River
Dor
Megiddo
Jezreel
Jordan River
Taanach
Ramoth-gilead
I S R A E L
Samaria
Tirzah
Plain of Sharon
Shechem
Succoth
Joppa
Aphek
Penuel
AMMON
Gedor
Rabbah
Bethel
Gezer
Jericho
Ashdod
Jerusalem
Heshbon
Ekron
Ashkelon
Gath
Lachish
Dead Sea
PHILISTINES
Gaza
Hebron
Dibon
En-gedi
Arnon River
J U D A H
MOAB
Beersheba
Arad
Kir-haresheth
Negeb
Zered River
Tamar
Bozrah
Kadesh-barnea
EDOM
Arabah
Teman
Copper Mines
Elath

Legend:

Divided Kingdom 10th cent. B.C.

Jeroboam II and Uzziah, mid 8th cent. B.C.

Israel at the time of Tiglath-Pileser III, 732 B.C.

Josiah, 639 B.C.

Border between Israel and Judah

Scale: 0 20 40 miles / 0 20 40 60 km

© Carta, Jerusalem

The palace at Samaria

Israelite inner wall
Israelite casemate wall
Palace of the "Ivory House"
Palace
Pool
Store house (Ostraca House)
Tower

0 50 yards
0 50 meters

13

THE WORLD
OF THE
GREEKS

CELTS

IBERIANS

LIGURIANS

Agathe ★
Massilia ★
Emporiae ★ Olbia ★

ETRUSCANS

Alalia ★
Rome ★

ILLYRIA

Danube River

THRACE

MACEDONIA

Adriatic Sea

Gadara ★
Abdera ★
Tingis ★

Tharros ★
Carales ★

Neapolis ★
Tarentum ★

Epidamnos ★

Abdera ★
Olynthos ★
Potidaea ★

Byzantium ★
Aenos ★

Od
Ap

Cartenna ★
Iol ★ Tipasa ★

Hippo
Regius ★

Tyrrhenian
Sea

MAGNA GRAECIA

Sybaris ★
Hipponium ★

Croton ★

EPIRUS

Abydos ★
Troy ★ M

LESBOS

Delphi ★

CHIOS

LYD
Phoca

Alexander the Great

Utica ★
Carthage ★

Motya ★
SICILY

Rhegium ★

*Ionian
Sea*

Athens ★
Corinth ★

IONIA

NUMIDIA

Hadrumetum ★

Syracuse ★

Sparta ★

DORIA

Miletus ★

Aegean Sea

R

Thapsus ★

MELITA

Knossos ★

CRETE

Mediterranean

Sabrata ★
Olea ★
Leptis ★

Cyrene ★
Tauchira ★ Barca ★

Apollonia ★

Euhesperides ★

CYRENAICA

LIBYA

Ale

EMPIRE OF ALEXANDER THE GREAT
(late 4th century B.C.)

MACEDONIA
Pella ★

Black Sea

Athens ★
Sparta ★

Sardes ★

Aral Sea

Caspian Sea

Bactra ★

Maracanda ★
Derbent ★
Drapsaca ★

*Mediterranean
Sea*

Thapsacus ★
Nisibis ★
Gaugamela ★
SYRIA Arbela ★

Meshed ★

Massaga ★

Alexandria ★
Tyre ★
Damascus ★

Rhagae ★

Cabura ★
Kandahar ★

Ammonium ★
Memphis ★
Heliopolis ★
Jerusalem ★

Babylon ★
Charax ★

Ecbatana ★
Susa ★ PERSIA
Persepolis ★

EGYPT

Red Sea

ARABIA

Golashkerd ★

Pura ★

Patala ★

▨	Former Persian Empire	
▨	Alexander's Empire	
→	Routes taken by Alexander's army	
▪	Cities founded by Alexander	

Scale: 0 — 400 — 800 miles / 0 — 400 — 800 km

© Carta, Jerusalem

	Greek sphere	▨ Phoenician-Punic sphere	▨ Rome c.300
••••• Boundary of Persian Empire, c.350 B.C.		— Major sea rou	

Scale: 0 — 100 — 200 — 300 — 400 miles / 0 — 200 — 400 — 600 km

*Alexander the Great
in battle*

14

Greek merchant ship, 6th century B.C.

Seleucus I

As far back as historical records go, the Greeks lived in city-states on the Greek mainland and islands. Three waves of migration into Greece have been envisaged: (1) the Ionians, (2) the Achaeans (with the Aeolians), and (3) the Dorians. The Dorian migration from the north (c. 1000 B.C.) is the only one to have survived in historical memory. Pressed by later migrants, the earlier settlers crossed the Aegean and settled on the west coast of Asia Minor. Prominent among these were the Ionians: it was by their name that the Greeks were known in Western Asia. The Old Testament name Javan (Hebrew—*yawan*) is identical with Ion. From the Aegean world, Greek colonists sailed farther afield to the shores of the Black Sea, Sicily and South Italy (which was called Magna Graecia, "Great Greece"), and southeastern France (including Marseille and the lower Rhone Valley).

The Greek city-states made common cause in resisting the Persian invasions under Darius I (490 B.C.) and his son Xerxes (480 B.C.). But in general they remained divided and often at war with one another until they were conquered one by one by Philip II of Macedonia (356–336 B.C.) and incorporated in his Graeco-Macedonian empire. Philip's son Alexander the Great (336–323 B.C.) embarked on a campaign of conquest which carried him up the Nile and east through Afghanistan to the Indus valley. The Persian Empire disintegrated before his advance, but Alexander's united empire which took its place did not outlive him. After his death his leading generals divided it among themselves. Of the succession kingdoms the two which figure most in biblical history were the kingdom of Ptolemy and his successors in Egypt (ruling from Alexander's city of Alexandria) and that of Seleucus and his successors in Western Asia (ruling from Antioch in Syria). The Jews were now under Greek instead of Persian sovereignty. Until 198 B.C. they were subject to the Ptolemies; then, after a defeat inflicted on the Ptolemaic army by Antiochus III, they were subject for over fifty years to the Seleucids.

Even if Alexander's empire did not retain its political unity, it established a cultural unity. The Greek language and way of life were carried through the whole area of Alexander's conquests. Judaea was not immune to this hellenizing influence, but those Jews who settled in large numbers in Alexandria, Antioch and other Greek cities, were thoroughly hellenized. They continued to worship the God of Israel, but their synagogue services were conducted in Greek, and for their benefit—in the first instance, for the benefit of the Alexandrian Jews—their scriptures were translated from Hebrew into Greek. This is the translation commonly called the Septuagint.

Antiochus III

The Emperor Augustus

Palestine is a shortened form of the name given to the country by the Greeks and Romans: Syria Palaestina. It perpetuates the name of the Philistines, one of the many elements in its earlier population. It was subject to the Persians until 332 B.C. Then it was incorporated in the empire of Alexander the Great, who set up governors in Samaria and Judaea. After Alexander's death (323 B.C.), Palestine became a bone of contention between the Ptolemies in Egypt and the Seleucids in Syria. The Ptolemies held it until 198 B.C.; in that year Antiochus III of Syria defeated Ptolemy V at Panion (modern Banyas), at one of the sources of the Jordan, and wrested Palestine from him.

Under the Ptolemies and Seleucids Palestine was hellenized, largely by the founding of several Greek cities on the Mediterranean seaboard and in the Jordan valley. The latter included the ten cities of the Decapolis (cf. Matthew 4:25; Mark 5:20; 7:31). Even the Aramaic-speaking areas were much influenced by Greek language and culture.

The taxation of the territory was managed by an efficient bureaucracy and proved burdensome to the inhabitants, especially when Antiochus III, after his defeat by the Romans at Magnesia, had to raise money to pay the crushing indemnity they imposed on him. His son, Antiochus IV (175–163 B.C.), suspecting the Judaeans of disloyalty to his dynasty, deprived them of their inherited privileges and even banned the practice of their religion. This precipitated a revolt, led by Judas Maccabaeus and his brothers, members of the Hasmonaean priestly family. Judas was a gifted guerrilla leader, and won a series of victories which led, at the end of 164 B.C., to the restoration of religious freedom and the rededication of the Jerusalem temple to the worship of the God of Israel. Twenty-two years later, the restoration of religious freedom was followed by the regaining of political freedom, and for seventy-nine years the independent Jewish state was governed by the Hasmonaean dynasty.

When the Roman general Pompey, reorganizing Western Asia after putting down Mithridates, king of Pontus, arrived in Syria, he was invited to intervene in a feud between two princes of the Hasmonaean family. His intervention meant the end of Jewish independence. He occupied the city and temple of Jerusalem in 63 B.C.

Under the Romans an Idumaean statesman, Antipater, and his son Herod increased their power in Judaea. They made themselves so indispensable to the Romans that at last the Roman senate conferred on Herod the title of king of the Jews. His reign (37–4 B.C.) proved oppressive to his subjects, but he maintained peace and retained the confidence of his Roman master. He was a great builder. He founded Sebaste on the site of the ancient Samaria, and constructed a great harbour-city at Caesarea on the Mediterranean Sea. His best-known building achievement was the restoration and enlargement of the temple in Jerusalem.

At his death in 4 B.C., the Emperor Augustus divided Herod's kingdom among three of his sons. Judaea (with Samaria) went to Archelaus, Galilee and Peraea to Antipas, and the territory east and northeast of the lake of Galilee to Philip. Philip and Antipas ruled their territories for many years, but Archelaus's subjects found his rule so harsh that Augustus deposed him in A.D. 6, and Judaea was constituted a Roman province.

Warship on wall of Jason's Tomb, Jerusalem

PALESTINE IN GRAECO-ROMAN TIMES

PHOENICIA
ITUREA

Sidon
Damascus
Tyre
Antiochia
Panias 198 B.C.
Mt. Hermon
Litani River
Seleucia
Raphon

Ptolemais
GALILEE
Taricheae
Lake Gennesaret
Hippus
Asochis
Sepphoris
Philoteria
Abila
Mt. Carmel
Geba
Gadara
Mt. Tabor
Yarmuk River

Dora
Strato's Tower
Scythopolis
Pella
Jordan River

SAMARIA
Samaria
Gerasa
Shechem
Jabbok River

Apollonia
Pegae
Gedor
PEREA
Joppa
Philadelphia
Lydda
Modiin
Jamnia 147 B.C.
Emmaus
Beth-horon 166 B.C.
Jericho
Azotus
JUDEA
Jerusalem
Kidron
Bethlehem
Medeba
Ascalon
Marisa
Beth-zur
Beth-zechariah 162 B.C.
Anthedon
Hebron
Dead Sea
Gaza
IDUMEA
Arnon River
Raphia 217 B.C.
Beersheba

Mediterranean Sea

Rhinocorura
Elusa
Zoar

NABATEANS

Coins of the Hasmoneans

JERUSALEM OF THE HASMONEANS
(early 1st century B.C.)

Temple
Hasmonean Palace
ACRA
OPHEL
Agora
Tyropoeon Valley
UPPER CITY
LOWER CITY
Kidron Valley
Valley of Hinnom

0   100   200   300 yards
0   100   200 m

Legend
Kingdom under Simon Maccabeus, 143–135 B.C.
Acquired by John Hyrcanus, 135–104 B.C.
Acquired by Judas Aristobulus, 104–103 B.C.
Acquired by Alexander Janneus, 103–76 B.C.
● Hellenistic city
Ptolemais City of importance

0   10   20   30   40 miles
0   20   40   60 km

17

© Carta, Jerusalem

The map shows labels including: HIBERNIA, BRITANNIA, Eburacum, Lindum, Aquae Sulis, Londinium, North Sea, Atlantic Ocean, GERMANIA, Rhine River, GALLIA, Lutetia, Mediolanum, Lugdunum, Burdigala, Vienna, Nemausus, Narbo, Massilia, Regina Castra, Vindobona, RAETIA, NORICUM, PANNONIA, Aquileia, Genua, ITALIA, Ancona, Rome, Neapolis, ILLYRICUM, DACIA, Danube River, MOESIA, THRACE, MACEDONIA, Brundisium, Thessalonica, ACHAIA, Athens, Corinth, SARMATIA, Olbia, Ponticapaeum, Black Sea, Byzantium, BITHYNIA AND PONTUS, Ancyra, Pergamum, PHRYGIA, Ephesus, LYCIA, CILICIA, Tarsus, CYPRUS, CRETE, HISPANIA, Toletum, Corduba, Tarraco, Valentia, Gades, MAURETANIA, Hippo Regius, AFRICA, Carthage, Syracuse, Mediterranean Sea, Leptis Magna, Cyrene, CYRENE, Alexandria, Memphis, EGYPT, Nile River

ROME (1st-3rd centuries A.D.)

Map inset labels: Circus of Hadrian, Tomb of Augustus, PINCIAN HILL, Castra Praetoria, Mausoleum of Hadrian, QUIRINAL HILL, Baths of Diocletian, Circus of Nero, VATICAN HILL, Pantheon, VIMINAL HILL, Theater of Pompey, ESQUILINE HILL, CAPITOLINE HILL, Imperial Fora, Capitol, Roman Forum, Baths of Trajan, Colosseum, PALATINE HILL, Circus Maximus, T. Divi Claudii, CAELIAN HILL, Baths of Caracalla, AVENTINE HILL, + Earliest Christian sites, 0 500 1000 1500 yards, 0 500 1000 m

There are few more fascinating stories in the world history than the development of a group of hill settlements on the left bank of the Tiber, about 15 miles from its mouth, into a city which gradually dominated its immediate neighbours, then became mistress of Italy, survived an almost fatal conflict with Carthage, was drawn into the affairs of Greece, Asia Minor, Syria and Egypt and, by the middle of the first century B.C., ruled the Mediterranean world.

The Romans appear in biblical history at the beginning of the second century B.C. In 198 B.C. they declared a protectorate over the Greek city-states and, when the Seleucid king Antiochus III invaded Greece six years later, they drove him out and followed him into his own kingdom, where he was heavily defeated by a Roman general at the battle of Magnesia (190 B.C.). This general, Scipio Asiaticus, figures in Daniel 11:18 as the "commander" who put an end to Antiochus's "insolence." In the rivalry between the Ptolemies and the Seleucids Rome, from then on, took the Ptolemies' side. When Judas Maccabaeus and his brothers revolted against the Seleucids in 167 B.C. and the following years, the Romans encouraged them.

In 133 B.C. the last king of Pergamum bequeathed his kingdom, which covered much of Western Asia Minor, to the Roman state; it became the Roman province of Asia. In 88 B.C. the king of Pontus (on the south shore of the Black Sea) expelled the Romans temporarily from Asia, but involved himself in a war with them which ended with his downfall twenty-five years later. By 63 B.C. the Romans found themselves obliged to reorganize the whole of Western Asia. Syria was constituted a Roman

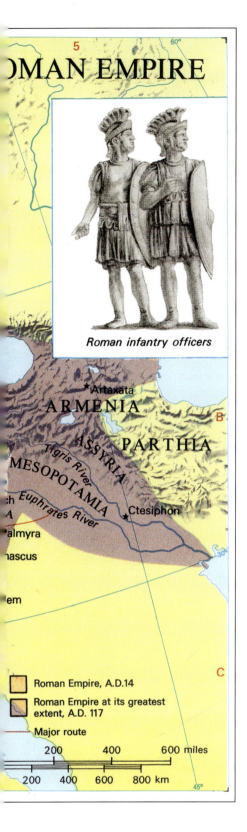

Roman infantry officers

*Artaxata
ARMENIA
ASSYRIA
PARTHIA
Tigris River
MESOPOTAMIA
Euphrates River
Ctesiphon
almyra
nascus
em

☐ Roman Empire, A.D.14
☐ Roman Empire at its greatest extent, A.D. 117
— Major route

200   400   600 miles

200   400   600   800 km

Roman warship

Captured Temple vessels; Arch of Titus, Rome

province; Judaea also became subject to Rome but for several decades continued to be governed by Jewish rulers, notably Herod the Great (37–4 B.C.) and his heirs.

After decades of civil war in Rome, Octavian (adopted son of Julius Caesar) defeated the last of his rivals in 31 B.C. and speedily established his position as undisputed head of the Roman Empire, with the title Augustus. He organized the empire from the English Channel to the Euphrates, making suitable provision for its defence. Those provinces which required the presence of a standing army were commanded by legates appointed directly by himself, like Quirinius in Syria (Luke 2:2). Augustus was commander-in-chief of all the Roman armies. Those provinces which were peaceful were governed by proconsuls appointed by the Roman senate, like Sergius Paulus in Cyprus (Acts 13:7) and Gallio in Achaia (Acts 18:12). So well organized was the empire that it survived periods of weakness and internal strife at the center, as at the assassination of the Emperor Gaius (A.D. 41) or the rise and fall of three short-lived emperors between the death of Nero and the accession of Vespasian (A.D. 68–69).

Jesus was born at Bethlehem in Judaea, some six miles south of Jerusalem, shortly before Herod's death, but he spent most of his life in Galilee. He was brought up at Nazareth, about four miles southeast of Sepphoris, which was until about A.D. 20 the residence of Herod Antipas, tetrarch of Galilee. Later, Antipas built himself a new capital at Tiberias, on the southwestern shore of the lake of Galilee.

The traditional sites of Jesus' baptism in the Jordan and his temptation in the wilderness are near Jericho. When he began his public ministry, he set up his headquarters at Capernaum, a Galilaean fishing town on the northwestern shore of the lake. Other towns which feature in the record of his Galilaean ministry are Cana, Nain, Chorazin and Bethsaida (which lies east of the point where the Jordan enters the lake from the north). When Herod Antipas, after his execution of John the Baptist, began to take an ominous interest in the activities of Jesus and his disciples, it was easy for them to sail across the lake and find refuge in the principality of his brother Philip. It was there that Jesus fed the multitudes and healed the Gadarene demoniac. It was in Philip's principality, too, near his capital Caesarea Philippi (modern Banyas), that Peter confessed Jesus to be the Messiah, a turning point in the gospel narrative.

Jesus paid several visits to Judaea, the direct road to which led through Samaria. His best-known experience in Samaria was his meeting with the woman of Sychar at Jacob's well, a well whose fresh water can be appreciated today (John 4:4–42).

When Jesus visited Judaea, he found himself in a Roman province, governed (from A.D. 26 to 36) by the prefect Pontius Pilate. A mutilated inscription bearing his name was discovered at Caesarea in 1961. For his last visit to Judaea, Jesus appears to have TRAVELED through Transjordan rather than Samaria, crossing the Jordan opposite Jericho. The road between Jericho and Jerusalem was the scene of the parable of the good Samaritan. Near the Jerusalem end of this road was the village of Bethany, where Jesus could count on the

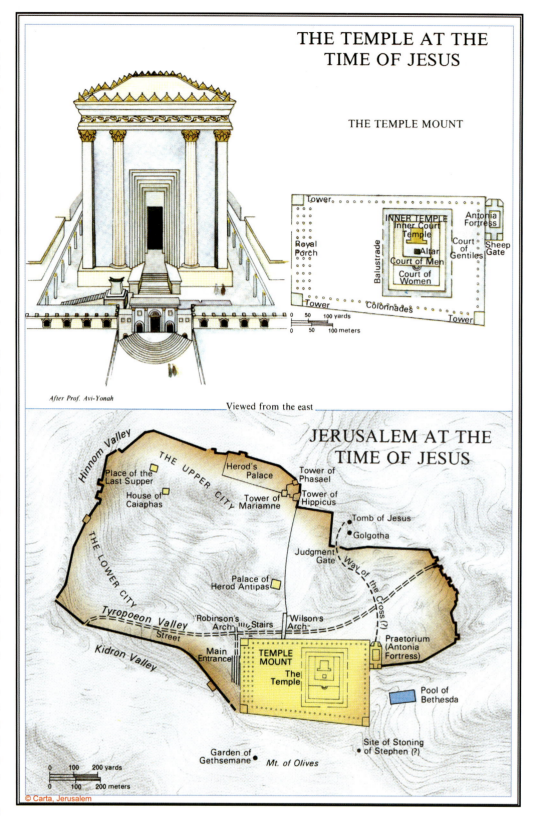

THE TEMPLE AT THE TIME OF JESUS

THE TEMPLE MOUNT

After Prof. Avi-Yonah

Viewed from the east

JERUSALEM AT THE TIME OF JESUS

© Carta, Jerusalem

hospitality of his friends Martha, Mary and Lazarus.

It was Pontius Pilate who sentenced Jesus to death by crucifixion. The Via Dolorosa in Jerusalem marks the traditional line of Jesus' brief journey from Pilate's judgment-hall (possibly in the Antonia fortress) to Golgotha. Golgotha lay by the main road just outside

a gate in the (second) north wall of the city; its site is covered by the Church of the Holy Sepulchre. There, on the third day, his tomb was found empty. In resurrection he appeared to his disciples at various places in Judaea and Galilee. His ascension traditionally took place from the location on the Mount of Olives called Viri Galilaei.

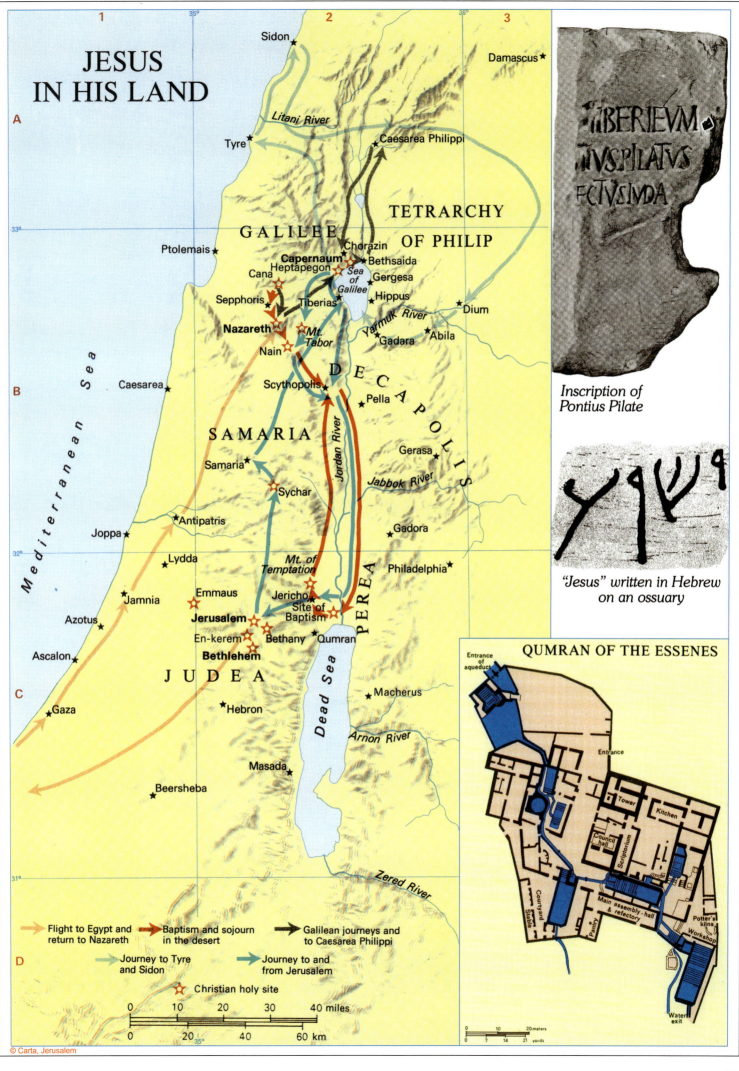

JESUS IN HIS LAND

Inscription of Pontius Pilate

TIBERIEVM
...TIVS.PILATVS
...FCTVS.IVDA...

"Jesus" written in Hebrew on an ossuary

Map labels

Sidon
Damascus
Litani River
Tyre
Caesarea Philippi
TETRARCHY
GALILEE
OF PHILIP
Ptolemais
Chorazin
Capernaum
Bethsaida
Heptapegon
Cana
Gergesa
Sea of Galilee
Sepphoris
Hippus
Tiberias
Yarmuk River
Dium
Nazareth
Mt. Tabor
Gadara
Abila
Nain
DECAPOLIS
Scythopolis
Caesarea
Pella
SAMARIA
Gerasa
Samaria
Jabbok River
Sychar
Jordan River
Antipatris
Joppa
Gadora
Lydda
Mt. of Temptation
Philadelphia
Emmaus
Jericho
Jamnia
PEREA
Jerusalem
Site of Baptism
En-kerem
Bethany
Qumran
Azotus
Bethlehem
JUDEA
Ascalon
Hebron
Macherus
Gaza
Masada
Dead Sea
Beersheba
Arnon River
Mediterranean Sea
Zered River

Legend

→ Flight to Egypt and return to Nazareth
→ Baptism and sojourn in the desert
→ Galilean journeys and to Caesarea Philippi
→ Journey to Tyre and Sidon
→ Journey to and from Jerusalem
✶ Christian holy site

0 10 20 30 40 miles
0 20 40 60 km

QUMRAN OF THE ESSENES

Entrance of aqueduct
Entrance
Tower
Kitchen
Council hall
Scriptorium
Courtyard
Stable
Main assembly-hall & refectory
Pantry
Potter's kilns
Workshop
Water exit

0 10 20 meters
0 7 14 21 yards

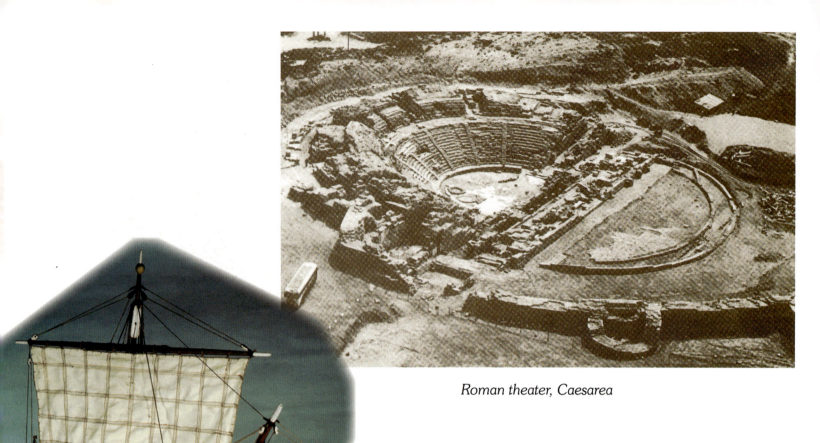

Roman theater, Caesarea

*Sidonian merchant ship,
2nd to 3rd cent. A.D.*

The map illustrates the narrative of Acts 1–12, covering a period of fifteen or sixteen years after the death and resurrection of Jesus (A.D. 30). To begin with, the main concentration of Jesus' disciples was the church of Jerusalem, although there were groups of disciples elsewhere, especially in Galilee and even as far north as Damascus. But about A.D. 33 a campaign of repression was launched by the authorities against the Hellenistic (Greek-speaking) members of the Jerusalem church, some of whom expressed sentiments which seemed to threaten the sanctity of the temple. They were forced to leave Jerusalem, and dispersed in every direction. Some traveled southwest and probably before long crossed the Egyptian frontier and carried the good news to Alexandria and farther west to Cyrene. But their activity is unchronicled.

We are more fully informed about others, who preached the gospel and planted Christian cells in the plain of Sharon and along the Mediterranean seaboard from Gaza to Caesarea. Yet others evangelized the cities farther north, including the seaports of Phoenicia (Lebanon). The disciples in Damascus had their ranks augmented by refugees from Jerusalem, and it was while he was in pursuit of those refugees that Saul of Tarsus (Paul the apostle) was converted to Christianity and became its most active propagator. After a brief mission among the Nabatean Arabs (east and south of Damascus), he visited the leaders of the Jerusalem church and then returned to his native Tarsus.

Meanwhile, the Hellenists who carried the gospel to the Phoenician cities continued their northward journey as far as Antioch in North Syria. There for the first time the gospel was preached to pagan Greeks. Many of these accepted the new faith and were incorporated in a mainly Gentile church. The apostles in Jerusalem sent Barnabas to direct this forward movement. He in turn fetched Paul from Tarsus to be his colleague in this work. About A.D. 46 news of a severe famine and food shortage in Judaea moved the converts in Antioch to send a gift of money for the relief of their fellow-Christians in Jerusalem. This set the pattern for the early practice of inter-church aid.

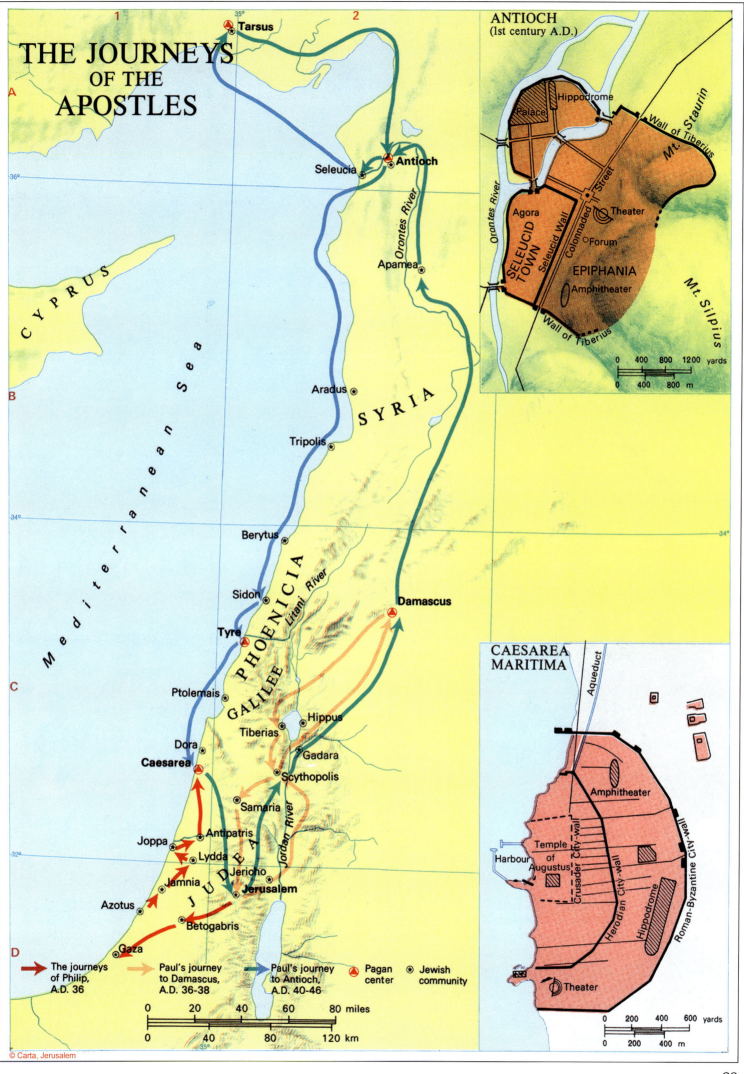

THE JOURNEYS OF THE APOSTLES

ANTIOCH (1st century A.D.)

Hippodrome
Palace
Wall of Staurin
Mt. Staurin
Orontes River
Agora
SELEUCID TOWN
Seleucid Wall
Colonnaded Street
Theater
Forum
EPIPHANIA
Amphitheater
Wall of Tiberius
Mt. Silpius

0 400 800 1200 yards
0 400 800 m

Tarsus

Seleucia Antioch

Orontes River

Apamea

CYPRUS

Aradus

SYRIA

Tripolis

Mediterranean Sea

Berytus

PHOENICIA

Litani River

Sidon

Damascus

Tyre

GALILEE

Ptolemais

Hippus

Tiberias

Dora

Gadara

Caesarea

Scythopolis

Samaria

Jordan River

Joppa Antipatris

Lydda

Jericho

Jamnia

JUDEA

Jerusalem

Azotus

Betogabris

Gaza

CAESAREA MARITIMA

Aqueduct

Amphitheater

Crusader City-wall

Temple of Augustus

Harbour

Herodian City-wall

Hippodrome

Roman-Byzantine City-wall

Theater

0 200 400 600 yards
0 200 400 m

→ The journeys of Philip, A.D. 36
→ Paul's journey to Damascus, A.D. 36-38
━ Paul's journey to Antioch, A.D. 40-46
⊙ Pagan center
✳ Jewish community

0 20 40 60 80 miles
0 40 80 120 km

© Carta, Jerusalem

23

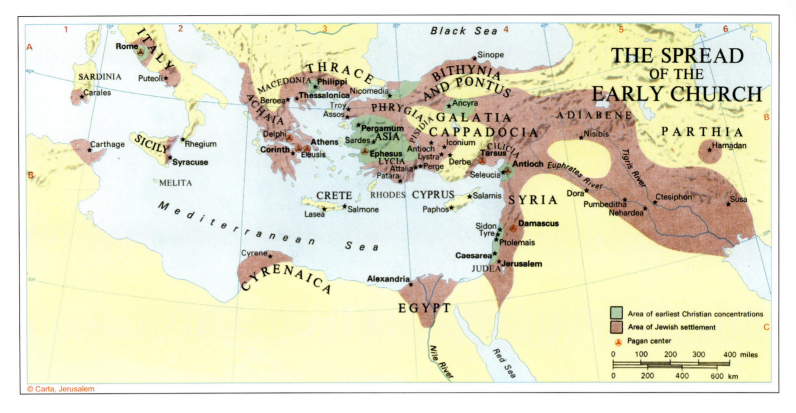

About A.D. 46 or 47 the church of Antioch released Barnabas and Paul for missionary work in Cyprus and Asia Minor. The churches of South Galatia in Pisidian Antioch, Iconium, Lystra and Derbe were founded at this time.

The growing influx of Gentiles into the church was seen as a threat by some Jewish Christians, and a meeting was convened at Jerusalem to consider if special conditions should be laid down for the admission of Gentiles. It was decided that they should be admitted on the same terms as Jewish believers, but they were urged to observe certain food restrictions and the like which would make it easier for Jewish Christians to have social fellowship with them (to eat at the same table, for example).

Paul, apostle-in-chief to the Gentile world, then embarked on two great campaigns of evangelization: the first in Macedonia and Achaia (Greece), which resulted in the planting of churches in Philippi, Thessalonica, Beroea and Corinth, and the second in Ephesus. For nearly three years (A.D. 52–55) Paul stayed in this city, and so effectively did he and his colleagues prosecute their work that the whole province of Asia heard the gospel and churches were established in all its chief cities. At the end of this period Paul briefly revisited Macedonia and Achaia, and then sailed for Judaea. He was accompanied by a number of representative Gentile Christians who carried money from their respective churches as a gift to the Jerusalem church.

In Jerusalem Paul was involved in a riot and was taken into custody by the Roman administration. He was sent to Rome to have his case heard by the emperor. His voyage there was interrupted by storm and shipwreck at Malta, where he spent the winter months of A.D. 59–60. In Rome he stayed for two years under house arrest, waiting for his case to come up for trial. His presence there was a great stimulus to the progress of the gospel in the capital. His execution was probably one incident in the persecution of Christians which broke out in the aftermath of the great fire of Rome (A.D. 64).

While Paul's career is documented fairly fully in the New Testament, there were other missionary enterprises among both Jews and Gentiles at whose course we can but guess. The gospel reached Rome, for example, long before any apostle visited the city. The map above illustrates the great expansion of Christianity in Mesopotamia and Iran, which in those days belonged to the Parthian empire. Between 170 and 180 there were Christian churches in and around Carthage, and also at Lyon and Vienna in the Rhone valley, which had been evangelized from the province of Asia.

Merchant ship of Roman period

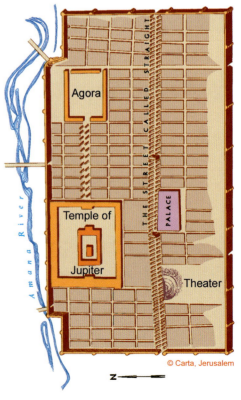

Damascus in the days of Paul

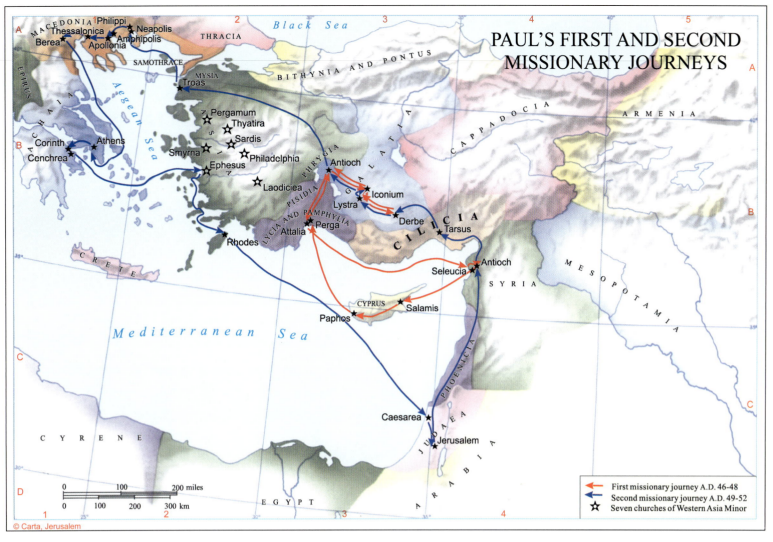

PAUL'S FIRST AND SECOND MISSIONARY JOURNEYS

First missionary journey A.D. 46-48
Second missionary journey A.D. 49-52
Seven churches of Western Asia Minor

© Carta, Jerusalem

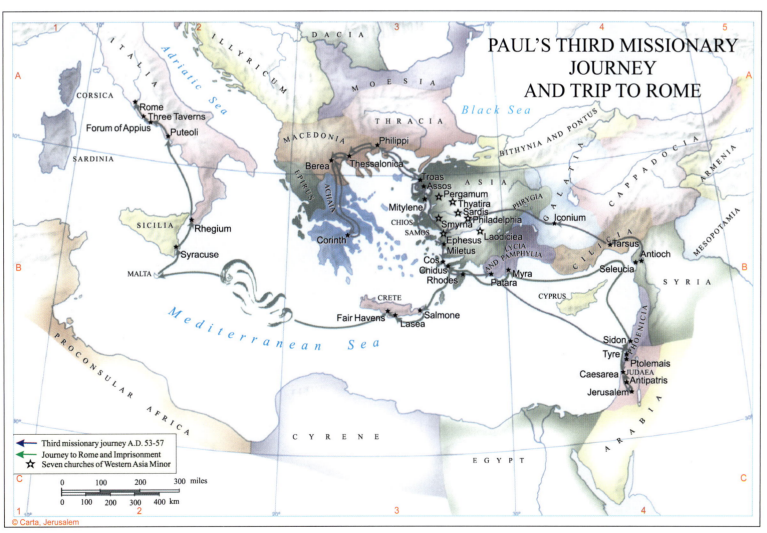

PAUL'S THIRD MISSIONARY JOURNEY AND TRIP TO ROME

Third missionary journey A.D. 53-57
Journey to Rome and Imprisonment
Seven churches of Western Asia Minor

© Carta, Jerusalem

25

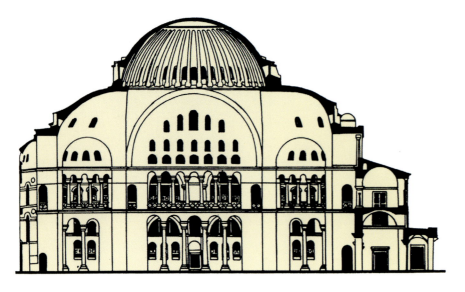

Hagia Sophia, Constantinople

Roman coast guard ship, 2nd cent. A.D.

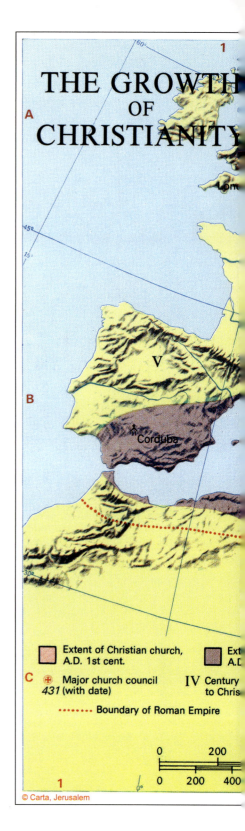

THE GROWTH
OF
CHRISTIANITY

Corduba

Extent of Christian church,
A.D. 1st cent.

Ext
A.D

⊕ Major church council
431 (with date)

IV Century
to Chris

······· Boundary of Roman Empire

0   200
0   200   400

© Carta, Jerusalem

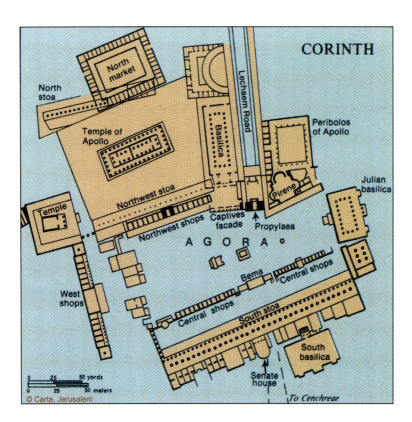

CORINTH

North
market

North
stoa

Temple of
Apollo

Basilica

Lechaem Road

Peribolos
of Apollo

Northwest stoa

Pirene

Julian
basilica

Temple

Northwest shops

Captives
facade

Propylaea

A G O R A

West
shops

Central shops

Bema

Central shops

South stoa

South
basilica

Senate
house

0   25   50 yards
0   25   50 meters
© Carta, Jerusalem

To Cenchreae

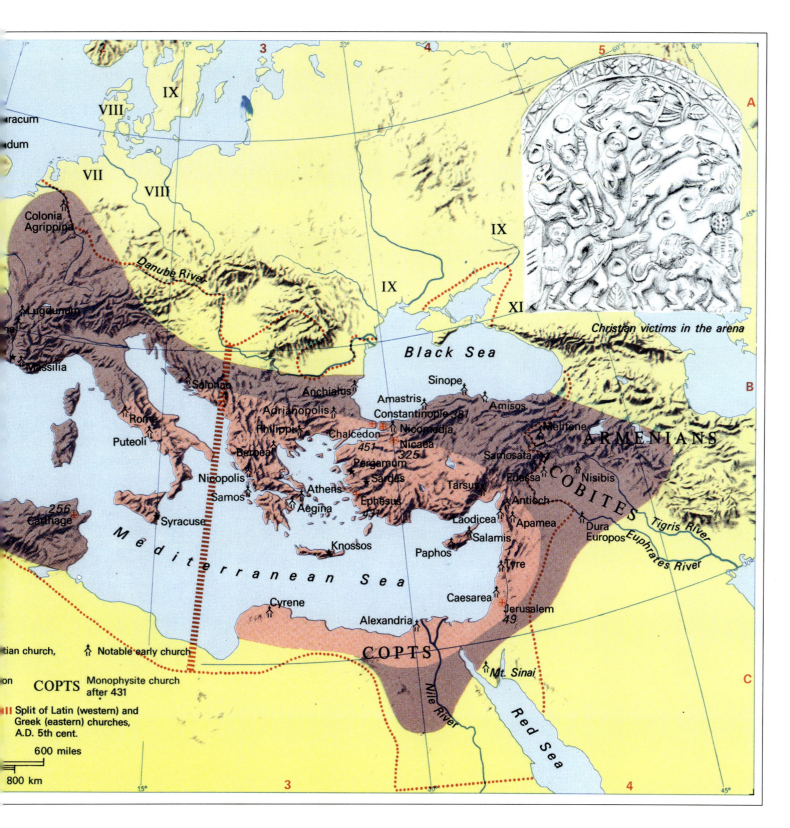

VIII

IX

racum

dum

VII

VIII

Colonia
Agrippina

Danube River

Lugdunum

Massilia

Salonae

Rome

Puteoli

Berbea

Philippi

Adrianopolis

Anchialus

Amastris

Constantinople 381

Nicomedia

Chalcedon
451

Nicaea
325

Black Sea

Sinope

Amisos

Melitene

ARMENIANS

Samosata

COBITES

Edessa

Nisibis

Tigris River

Euphrates River

Nicopolis

Samos

Athens

Aegina

Sardes

Pergamum

Ephesus

Tarsus

Antioch

Laodicea

Apamea

Dura
Europos

IX

XI

Christian victims in the arena

Syracuse

256
Carthage

Knossos

Paphos

Salamis

Tyre

Mediterranean Sea

Cyrene

Alexandria

Caesarea

Jerusalem
49

COPTS

Mt. Sinai

Nile River

Red Sea

tian church,

Notable early church

COPTS Monophysite church
after 431

Split of Latin (western) and
Greek (eastern) churches,
A.D. 5th cent.

600 miles

800 km

In the period illustrated in this map, Christianity was not only established in the regions shown, but secured the allegiance of the rulers of various states, including Edessa (modern Urfa), east of the Upper Euphrates (soon after A.D. 200), and Armenia (about A.D. 300). The Roman Empire first permitted Christians the free exercise of their religion in A.D. 313 (under Constantine); Christianity (orthodox Christianity at that) became the sole authorized religion of the empire under Theodosius (A.D. 381). How soon Christianity came to Britain is unknown; by 314 it was sufficiently well established for three British bishops (those of London, Lincoln and York) to attend a church council at Arelate (Arles) in the south of France.

The Syriac-speaking churches east of the Euphrates advanced the frontiers of Christianity down the Persian Gulf to the coast of India and overland through Central Asia until in due course it penetrated China.

When Britain was invaded and occupied by barbarians from the continent (from A.D. 450 onward), these had to be evangelized in turn. Their evangelization was effected by two missions: a Roman mission in the south, led by Augustine of Canterbury (who arrived in 597), and an Irish mission in the north, led by Aidan, who came from Iona and settled in Lindisfarne in 635. (Ireland had been evangelized, mainly by Patrick, between 432 and 461; Iona was an outpost of Irish Christianity.) From christianized England the gospel was carried to Frisia and northwestern Germany.

ISRAEL
Incl. Palestinian Autonomous Areas

Mediterranean Sea

LEBANON

Nahariya
Ma'alot-Tarshiha
Akko (Acre)
Kiryat Shmona
Hatzor Haglilit
Golan
Galilee
Safad
Karmi'el
Sakhnin
Araba
Kiryat Yam
Kiryat Motzkin
Haifa
Shfar'am
Tiberias
Lake Kinneret
Tirat Carmel
Kiryat Ata
Isfiya
Daliyat el Carmel
Kiryat Tivon
Nazareth
Natzrat Ilit
Yokne'am
Migdal Ha'emek
Afula
Afula Ilit
Zichron Ya'akov
Binyamina
Pardes Hana-Karkur
Kafr Qari'
Umm el Fahm
Beit She'an
Giv'at Olga
Arara
Jenin
Baka al Gharbiya
Kabatiya
Hadera
Samaria
Netanya
Tubas
Tulkarm
Tira
Taiyba
Ra'anana
Kalkilya
Herzliya
Kfar Sava
Shechem (Nablus)
Hod Hasharon
Ramat Hasharon
Ramat Gan
Rosh Ha'ayin
Ari'el
Tel Aviv - Yafo
Kiryat Ono
Petah Tikva
Bat-Yam
Yehud
Or Yehuda
Ben-Gurion Airport
Holon
Lod
Rishon Lezion
Ramla
Modi'in
Ramallah
Nes Ziona
Maccabim
Re'ut
Rehovot
El Bira
Yavneh
Jericho
Ashdod
Ma'aleh Adumim
Gedera
Mevaseret Zion
Kiryat Malachi
Jerusalem
Ashkelon
Beit Shemesh
Beit Jala
Bethlehem
Beit Sahur
Gaza
Judea
Kiryat Gat
Sderot
Halhul
Kiryat Arba
Deir el Balah
Hebron
Khan Yunis
Rahat
Rafi'ah
Ofakim
Arad
Judean Desert
Dead Sea
Jordan Valley
Be'er Sheva
Dimona
J O R D A N
S Y R I A
Yeroham
Great Crater
N e g e v
Mitzpeh Ramon
Ramon Crater
A r a v a
E G Y P T
Sinai
Eilat
Akaba
Gulf of Eilat

Legend:
■■■ International boundary
Lines of separation-of-forces, 1974

Palestinian autonomous areas:
■ Area A
■ Area B

■ Green Area/Nature Reserve

0 10 20 30 km
0 10 20 miles

© Carta, Jerusalem

SATELLITE VIEW
OF THE
HOLY LAND

28

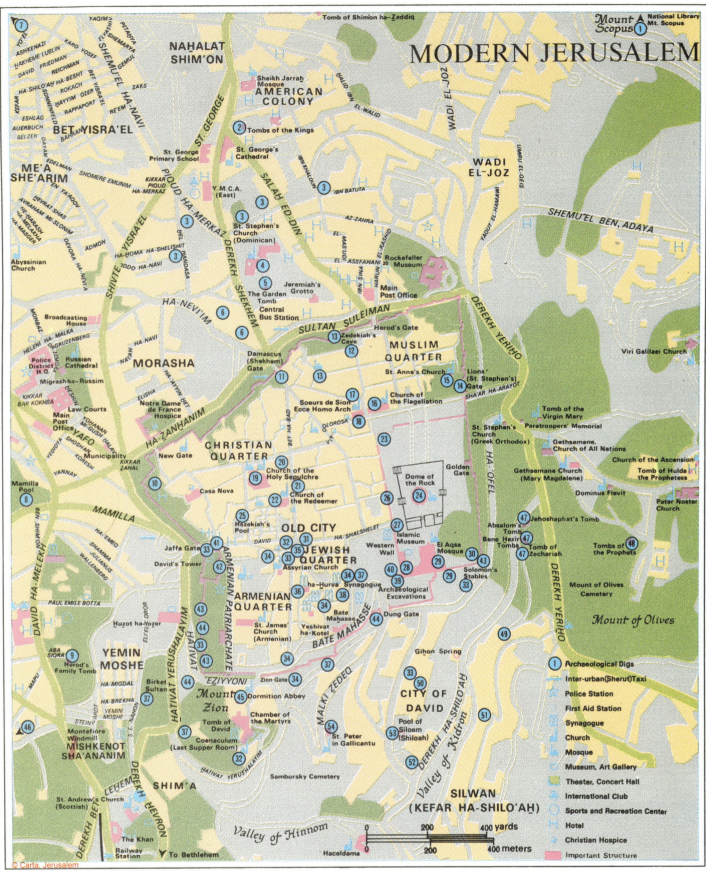

ARCHAE-OLOGICAL DIGS AND REMAINS FROM OLD AND NEW TESTAMENT TIMES

1 Second Temple tombs
2 "Tomb of the Kings"
3 Remains of Third Wall
4 First Temple tombs
5 Garden Tomb
6 First Temple period tombs
7 Sanhedrin tombs
8 Mamilla Pool
9 Tomb of Herod's Family
10 Remains of Third Wall
11 Wall and gate, Second Temple period
12 "Solomon's Quarries"
13 "Zedekiah's Cave"
14 Sitti Maryam (Mary's) Pool
15 Sheep Pools
16 Struthion Pools
17 First Temple period tombs
18 Ecce Homo Arch
19 Second Temple period tombs
20 Second Temple period wall
21 Second Temple period wall
22 First Temple period remains
23 Second Temple enclosure remains
24 "Foundation Stone"
25 Hezekiah's Pool
26 Warren's Gate
27 Wilson's Arch
28 Temple enclosure remains
29 Huldah (Double) and Single Gates
30 "Solomon's Stables"
31 Hellenistic tower
32 Wall and gate, Second Temple period
33 Building, First Temple period
34 Building, Second Temple period
35 Israelite tower and building
36 Hezekiah's wall
37 Lower aqueduct
38 Building and pool
39 Robinson's Arch
40 Temple enclosure remains
41 Tower of Hippicus
42 Towers and building
43 Second Temple period walls
44 First Temple period toms
45 "House of Caiaphas"
46 Jason's Tomb
47 Tombs/monuments: "Absalom," Zechariah, Bene Hezir
48 "Tombs of the Prophets"
49 Gihon Spring, Jebusite wall
50 First Wall remains
51 "Tomb of Pharaoh's Daughter"
52 Siloam Pool
53 Second Temple period cisterns
54 Second Temple period tombs

CHRONOLOGICAL TABLE

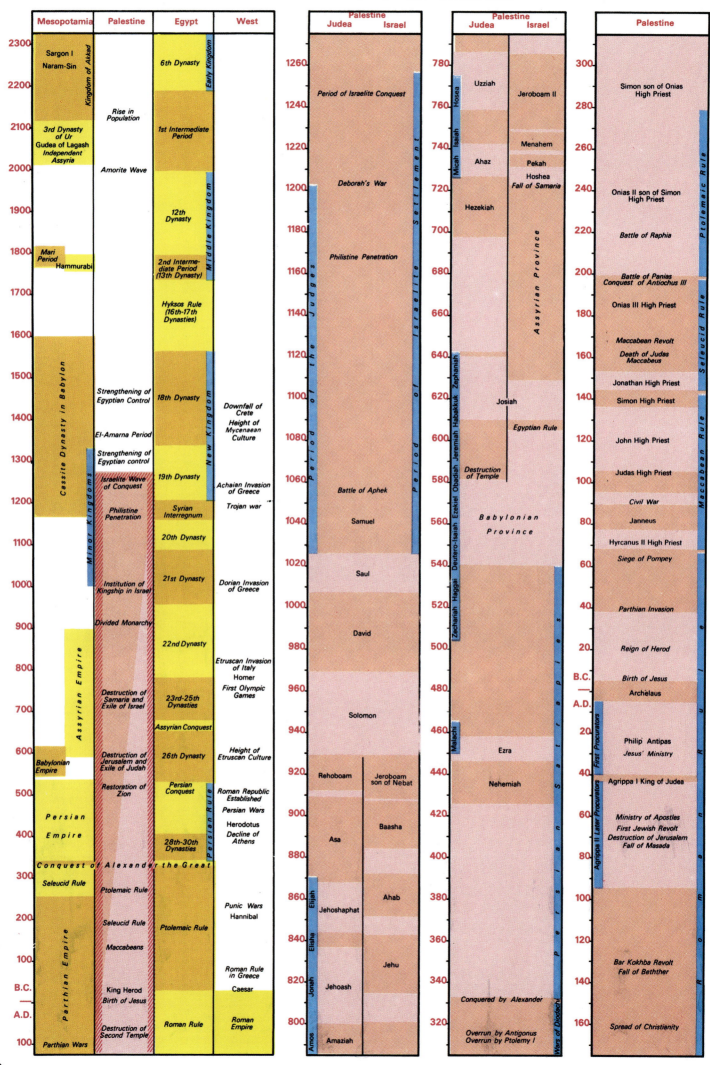

INDEX TO MAPS

* = Inset

31